ANIMAL SNACKERS

ANIMAL SNACKERS

BETSY LEWIN

SCHOLASTIC INC.
New York Toronto London Auckland Sydney
Mexico City New Delhi Hong Kong Buenos Aires

ISBN 0-439-77357-1

Text copyright © 1980 by Betsy Lewin. Illustrations copyright © 2004 by Betsy Lewin. Revised text copyright © 2004 by Betsy Lewin. *Animal Snackers* was originally published in 1980 by Dodd, Mead and Company. All rights reserved. Published by Scholastic Inc., 557 Broadway, New York, NY 10012, by arrangement with Henry Holt and Company, LLC. SCHOLASTIC and associated logos are trademarks and/or registered trademarks of Scholastic Inc.

12 11 10 9 8 7 6 5 4 3 2 1   5 6 7 8 9 10/0

Printed in the U.S.A.   40

First Scholastic printing, November 2005

Design by Patrick Collins

The artist used brush and ink on tracing paper, then copied those drawings onto Strathmore paper and used watercolors to create the illustrations for this book.

To all creatures furred,
feathered, and scaled

Just Imagine

Imagine if we all could eat
nothing but our favorite treat,

eating where and when we're able,
never seated at a table.

GORILLA

Gorillas, though they look like brutes,
may snack on tender bamboo shoots.

The sight of them may shiver us,
but they are not carnivorous.

PLATYPUS

The platypus looks odd enough,
with fur and ducklike bill.

He thinks that bugs are yummy stuff,
which makes him odder still.

OSTRICH

The ostrich eyes with eager glint
a stone—his after-dinner mint.

It is a snack that he must swallow
so indigestion does not follow.

KOALA

Koalas decorate the trees,
munching eucalyptus leaves.

This isn't just their favorite treat—
it is the only thing they eat.

PUFFIN

The puffin dives for little fish
with feats of derring-do,

then feeds its chick the tasty dish—
the chick likes herring, too.

ANTEATER

Eating ants is tricky,
but his tongue is long and sticky.

His snout is like a hose.
He just sucks ants up his nose.

TICKBIRD

Tickbirds ride the rhino's back,
looking for a tasty snack.

The rhino tolerates these guests
because they rid him of his pests.

RACCOON

Raccoons are not a fussy clan
when it comes time to eat.

They'll even raid a garbage can
to find a midnight treat.

FRUIT BAT

Fruit bats hanging by their feet
select some purple figs to eat.

This puzzles me and makes me frown.
How do they do it upside down?

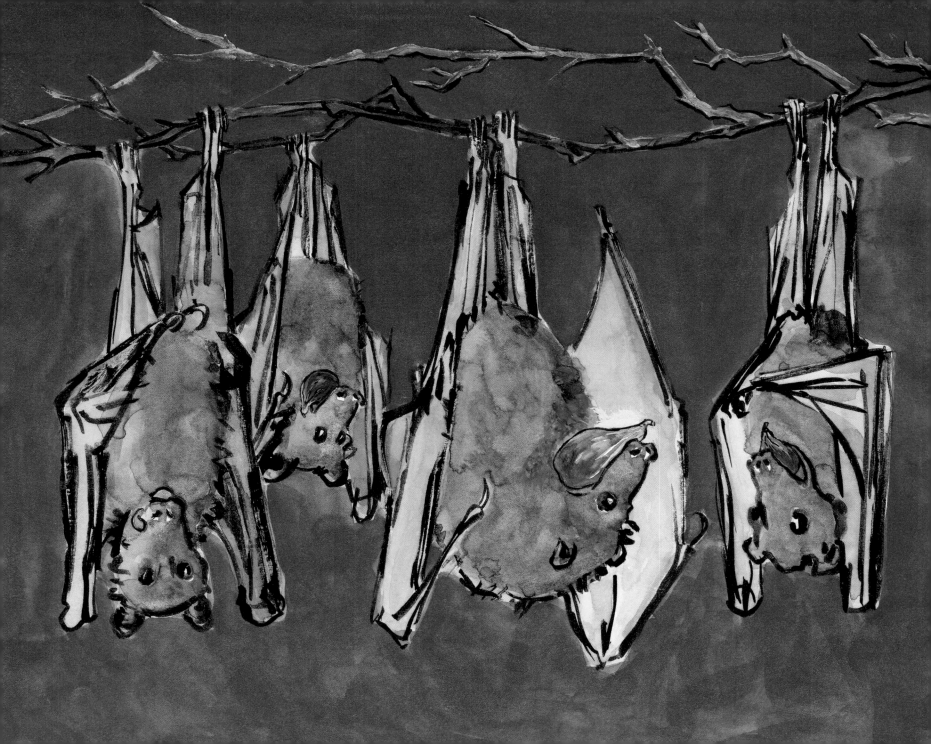

SEA OTTER

The sea otter really prefers to recline
on his waterproof back in the kelp and the brine.

Abalone and clams are his favorite snacks.
He hammers each shell on a stone till it cracks.

PORCUPINE

The porcupine is apt to dine
on twigs and bark—I think that's fine.

Such woody snacks I will decline
and leave them for the porcupine.

CROCODILE

Some fishes swimming in the Nile
ignore the hungry crocodile.

They would do well to watch their backs
or risk becoming croco-snacks.

ANIMAL FACTS

ANTEATER (South America) ✦ The giant anteater is the size of a German shepherd dog and can eat 30,000 insects a day. Its tongue is two feet long.

CROCODILE (Africa) ✦ Crocodiles like to eat often, but they can go without food for many days, or maybe even a whole year!

FRUIT BAT (South America) ✦ All bats have special tendons in their feet that lock the toes in a curled position so they can hang upside down without using muscle energy. They must flex their muscles to let go.

GORILLA (Africa) ✦ An adult male gorilla eats up to 40 pounds of vegetation a day.

KOALA (Australia) ✦ Koalas rarely drink water. They get all they need from eucalyptus leaves, which are 50 percent water. The word *koala* in the aboriginal language means "no drink."

OSTRICH (Africa) ✦ The ostrich is the world's largest living bird. It grows up to eight feet tall.

PLATYPUS (Australia) ✦ The male platypus has a poisonous spur on each of its hind legs that it uses to defend itself against predators.

PORCUPINE (North America) ✦ Porcupine quills are actually modified hairs that are loosely attached to the animal's body.

PUFFIN (Atlantic Coast) ✦ A puffin usually carries four or five herring, pushing each fish to the back of its bill with its tongue as it catches the next one. But, depending on the size of the fish, it has been known to carry more than 20 fish at a time.

RACCOON (Canada to South America) ✦ Raccoons are great survivors. They are omnivorous, which means they'll eat both meat and vegetables, including, of course, garbage.

SEA OTTER (Pacific Coast) ✦ Sea otters wrap themselves in seaweed so they won't drift away while they're sleeping. They sleep on their backs and, if it's daytime, sometimes cover their eyes with their paws. They are the only mammals other than primates that are known to use tools.

TICKBIRD (Africa) ✦ Tickbird is a nickname for the oxpecker. Oxpeckers and their hosts, which include oxen, deer, giraffes, and elephants, in addition to rhinos, are symbionts—two different species that benefit from living together.